GW00382180

TO

Angela

FROM

Mary

with love ..

DATE

12th December 2003

MESSAGE

Wishing you a very happy birthday ~
with many thanks for your sharing
in ministry, for your caring & love —
with my love & prayers for the Lord's
ongoing anointing & joy in your life —
        Thank you for being you ..

PRAYERS
AND
MEDITATIONS

A DEVOTIONAL OF CLASSIC PRAYERS

christian
art gifts

Prayers and Meditations

© 2003 Christian Art Gifts, PO Box 1599, Vereeniging, 1930, South Africa
© 2003 Christian Art Gifts, Illinois, USA

Devotions written by Lynette Douglas
Designed by Christian Art Gifts

Scripture taken from the HOLY BIBLE, NEW INTERNATIONAL VERSION®. NIV® Copyright© 1973, 1978, 1984 by
International Bible Society. Used by permission of Zondervan Publishers House.
All rights reserved.

ISBN 1-86920-058-6

Printed in China

03   04   05   06   07   08   09   10   11   12   –   10   9   8   7   6   5   4   3   2   1

PRAYERS
AND
MEDITATIONS

CONTENTS

THE LORD'S PRAYER

This most well-known of prayers deserves careful consideration from anyone desiring to embark on or deepen a life of prayer. It was the pattern Jesus laid down when His disciples asked Him, "Lord, teach us to pray." While learning it by heart is beneficial to the soul, it was not the intention of Jesus that this, or any prayer, be used simply as a recitation. Its power and effectiveness lie in the scope it provides for the one who prays. Allow your own thoughts and words to permeate the flow of the prayer.

This is a complete prayer, covering every aspect of life. It is indeed the classic primer in the School of Prayer. Prayer starts with worship, with coming before God, believing that He is and that He rewards those who diligently seek Him (Heb. 11:6). We confess that the Kingdom of Heaven is near at hand, and that its rule and authority are available to respond to our prayers. And because we focus on the Kingdom of Heaven, we pray too that the will of God will be done in every situation we bring before Him. We pray according to the will of God, knowing that as we do so, we will have whatever we ask. We intercede before God with the confidence of knowing He will fulfill His purposes on earth as He does in heaven (1 Jn. 5:14-15).

With the same confidence, we petition Him for our own daily needs, knowing that each day has its unique circumstances, and His grace is sufficient for our every day. Once we have the surety of His answers, we are conscious of our own sinfulness, and seek His forgiveness, allowing His forgiveness to extend through us to others. We ask for protection from evil, and end with the praise of knowing God has heard us.

Our Father which art in heaven, hallowed be Thy name. Thy kingdom come. Thy will be done on earth, as it is in heaven. Give us today our daily bread. And forgive us our trespasses, as we forgive them who trespass against us. And lead us not into temptation, but deliver us from evil. For Thine is the kingom, and the power and the glory for ever.

True repentance is birthed in a realization of the wretchedness of our sinful state in contrast with the holiness of God. No matter what we do – whether the obvious "big" sins which David repents of here, or tiny almost imperceptible sins – sin separates us from God, because nothing evil can come before Him. Sinfulness is falling short of the glory of God (Rom. 3:23), and if we desire to please Him, if our lives are governed by His love, then anything that dims our view of Him should bring us to deep sorrow and repentance.

David knew that he had wronged many people through his deeds, but he realized that it was against God that he had sinned, and that only God could cleanse and restore him. There is nothing that we can do that God cannot forgive if we turn to Him with penitent hearts. It is only God who can remove the guilt of our sin, and so, when we come to Him in prayer, and find Him separated from us, allow Him to search our hearts and find the things which are sinful, and then let Him renew our spirits.

Not only can God wash away our sins with the most powerful substance – the Blood of Jesus – the only thing capable of washing away the stain of sin on our souls, making our hearts clean – but He makes them pure and holy too. And as His purity floods through us, our hearts are strengthened and we are able to withstand further sinful onslaughts with a heart willing to follow God's ways. So, let us daily confess our sins, submit to Him, and His joy will fill us anew and sustain us.

Have mercy on me, O God, according to your unfailing love; according to your great compassion blot out my transgressions. Wash away all my iniquity and cleanse me from my sin. Surely you desire truth in the inner parts; you teach me wisdom in the inmost place. Create in me a pure heart, O God, and renew a steadfast spirit within me. Do not cast me from your presence or take your Holy Spirit from me. Restore to me the joy of your salvation and grant me a willing spirit, to sustain me.

Psalm 51:1-2, 6, 10

AN IRISH BLESSING

To be able to bless others is a privilege we little understand. To ask for God's favor on them, to pray for God to fill their lives with pleasant things, to see God's hand protect and guide them – are all delights that can be the result of our prayers for others. Often we intone the words, "God bless you" without considering the specific ways in which God's blessing can enrich the lives of those we love.

The Christian life is a journey through a foreign land to our eternal home. And on the journey we encounter many difficulties: unpleasant weather, steep and rocky paths, unknown territory and unforeseen dangers. This traditional blessing prays for God's protection of the pilgrim on his way through life. If we are always safe in God's hand, then nothing can happen to us that will overcome us or lead us away from the right road. With God as our guide, each day is filled with beauty, joy and peace. The road rises to meet us, making our walk easy. We don't need to fight against the wind, or the elements that come our way, for God will position them in such a way that they encourage and strengthen us and help us move forward confidently through life. God will protect us from the harshness of the sun by day and the moon by night. Rains will fall into every life, but those who are protected by God find the rains a blessing. They fall in their proper season and cause growth and provide nourishment.

Wherever the road through life leads us, we can know that God is with us. And He will bring us safely home, where we will meet again all those whom we have loved and blessed.

May the road rise to meet you,

may the wind be always at your back,

may the sun shine warm on your face,

the rain fall softly on your fields;

and until we meet again, may God

hold you in the palm of His hand.

God invites us to bring all our concerns and anxieties and worries to Him. He asks us to pray to Him because He longs to be involved in every aspect of our lives. Yes, He could simply provide for all our needs before we pray. After all, He knows every word we speak before we speak it! But then we would not need to know Him intimately. And He created us to have fellowship with Him. When we surrender our lives to Jesus and are born again, He takes up residence in our hearts, and the depths of our souls call out to Him. Then we call to Him and He answers us – He lavishes His blessings upon us.

He heals us from every physical and emotional disease. He forgives us no matter what wrong we do or what right we neglect to do. He redeems our lives from the pits of despair, of worldliness, of egoism, of debauchery, of sin. He replaces our rags of self-centeredness with robes of righteousness and He crowns us with love and compassion. The Bible overflows with the love of God towards us. On every page we are overwhelmed by the splendor of His love for us, of the mercies He pours out for us. His compassions reach out to us in our pitiful state, in our weariness and destitution, and lift us up to heavenly places with Him where our desires are fully satisfied and our youth is renewed.

He gives us all these things though we do not deserve them – simply because of the love He has for us which was expressed fully in the death of Jesus on the cross. When we consider all the wonders of God, all that He has so graciously and unstintingly given us, our inmost beings are stirred, and from deep within our souls we praise Him.

Praise the LORD O my soul;
all my inmost being,
praise his holy name.
Praise the LORD, O my soul,
and forget not all his benefits –
who forgives all your sins
and heals all your diseases,
who redeems your life from the pit
and crowns you with love
and compassion, who satisfies
your desires with good things,
so that your youth is
renewed like the eagle's.

Psalm 103:1-5

15

How often do we long to be in heaven, to know without a doubt that all prayers are heard and answered, that God's will is always done! The Bible describes our prayers as rising to God with the smoke of incense (Rev. 8:3-4), a rich image of purity and holiness as prayers are offered in fragrant sacrifice to God before His throne. How thrilling it is to know that heaven is a real place, and that God reigns there, and in our lives and that our prayers are heard and answered.

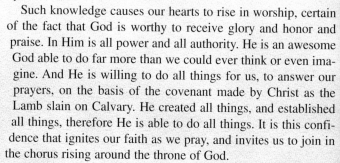

Such knowledge causes our hearts to rise in worship, certain of the fact that God is worthy to receive glory and honor and praise. In Him is all power and all authority. He is an awesome God able to do far more than we could ever think or even imagine. And He is willing to do all things for us, to answer our prayers, on the basis of the covenant made by Christ as the Lamb slain on Calvary. He created all things, and established all things, therefore He is able to do all things. It is this confidence that ignites our faith as we pray, and invites us to join in the chorus rising around the throne of God.

When we feel disheartened because we cannot see how our prayers can be answered, it is good to meditate on the glory of God, finding in Him a cause to celebrate. Very soon our worship will intermingle with our prayers, and we too will declare *You are worthy, our Lord and God.*

*You are worthy, our Lord and
God, to receive glory and honor
and power, for you created all
things, and by your will they
were created and have their being.*

*Worthy is the Lamb, who was slain,
to receive power and wealth
and wisdom and strength and
honor and glory and praise!*

*To him who sits on the throne and
to the Lamb be praise and
honor and glory and
power, for ever and ever!*

Revelation 4:11, 5:12-13

God is busy working within us so that we will reflect the image of Christ in the world around us. He has called us with a holy calling to be transformed into His likeness and therefore to be like Jesus in every situation we encounter in life. Wherever we are, as we yield to Him, allowing Him to wash away the hard corners of our heart, and filling us with His Holy Spirit we become more and more like Him.

In many ways this prayer of Francis of Assisi captures the essence of the Sermon on the Mount. As we pray that God fill us with the fruit of the Spirit, and as they grow in us, we become people who seek the good of others, who will go the second mile, who will love our enemies, and our friends! Who will not despair at the sinfulness of others, but who will seek to bring the principles of God's Kingdom to reign in every life we encounter.

The most powerful way of overcoming every outworking of evil is to come against it in the opposite spirit – where hatred and bitterness wreak havoc, we bring the healing power of love; where darkness and despair cause disillusionment, the light of Christ brings hope and vision. Instead of responding to persecution with retaliation, we pardon and forgive and love, bringing Christ's hope to others. Then we live as Christians in a lost world, sowing the seeds that will bear the fruits of righteousness. This prayer, sincerely prayed, will help us grow into the kind of people God can use as instruments of His goodness and peace.

LORD, make me an instrument of Your peace. Where there is hatred, let me sow love, where there is injury, pardon, where there is doubt, hope, where there is darkness, light, where there is sadness, joy.

O Divine Master, grant that I may not so much seek to be consoled as to console, not so much to be understood as to understand, not so much to be loved as to love; for it is in giving that we receive, it is in pardoning that we are pardoned, it is in dying, that we awake to eternal life.

God is faithful to His Word, faithful to all His promises and faithful to Himself. He is perfect in faithfulness. When He makes a promise to us and establishes His covenant with us, He does so on the strength of His own faithfulness and His own unchangeableness (Heb. 6:13-18). It is because of these attributes of God that we can be confident when we bring our prayers to Him, trusting Him who cannot be untrue to Himself. His plans, which He established long ago, for each of us, will come to pass. The works of His hands are marvelous indeed.

As we pray, it is good to write down the answers we receive from God, so that we do not forget the great things He has done. And when we feel discouraged, remembering such things will encourage us to continue praying. Then our minds will be steadfast, unshaken by the vagaries of life. We will trust in Him forever and His peace will guard our hearts and our minds in every situation. We trust Him, because we know that He has heard us in the past, and therefore will continue to hear us, because His faithfulness lasts forever. Our prayers will be permeated with praise to Him, and we will come to Him in the perfect assurance that He hears our prayers and answers when we call.

O LORD, you are my God;
I will exalt you and praise your
name, for in perfect faithfulness you
have done marvelous things, things
planned long ago. You will keep in
perfect peace him whose mind is
steadfast, because he trusts in you.
Trust in the LORD forever; for the
LORD, the LORD, is the Rock eternal.

Isaiah 25:1, 26:3-4

PAUL'S PRAYER FOR THE PHILIPPIANS

This prayer of Paul's for the Christians in Philippi, sums up the qualities of Christianity which sets it apart from any other way of living the world may present. It is a prayer which illustrates a loving Christian community in action. Paul prays that love may increase amongst believers, and increased love is an indication of unity, for where we love with the same love with which Christ loved us, we will have the same purpose and will work together in harmony, and then the world will know that we are His disciples. We increase in love and knowledge of God, growing from glory to glory day by day as we allow God to work in us according to His good purposes (Phil. 2:13).

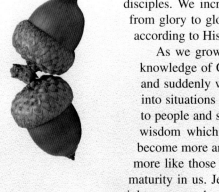

As we grow in love both for God and for each other, our knowledge of God – His nature and His will – also increases, and suddenly we find that we have insight and understanding into situations around us. We find that we are able to respond to people and situations with deeper understanding and with a wisdom which comes from God. Our motives and attitudes become more and more pure and our actions become more and more like those of Jesus as the fruit of righteousness comes to maturity in us. Jesus said that if we seek His kingdom and His righteousness above all other things, then we will have whatever we ask of God in prayer (Mt. 6:33). This righteousness comes through Christ, through our yielding to Him and seeking Him in prayer and worship. It is not a righteousness which comes from ourselves – for it is Christ alone who is righteous, and who imparts His righteousness to us. And as we grow in love, knowledge and righteousness, others will see and God will be praised.

And this is my prayer:

that your love may abound

more and more in knowledge and

depth of insight, so that you may be

able to discern what is best and may

be pure and blameless until the day

of Christ, filled with the fruit of

righteousness that comes through

Jesus Christ – to the

glory and praise of God.

Philippians 1:9-11

The Lord is the Good Shepherd who protects His sheep, leading them along the quiet paths of life, and refreshing them with still waters. His way is a way of peace and serenity. We walk in safety when we follow Him because He protects us from all dangers, from all who would harm us, if we remain near to Him. But if we do stray from the safe path of His will, we have His assurance that He will seek for the one who is lost, and will not rest until the lost lamb is safely back in His fold. His sheep know His voice and follow Him, and will not follow a stranger (Jn. 10:4). We have the privilege of knowing our Shepherd intimately, and it is in times of prayer that we learn to recognize His voice. Then we can know that as we live our daily lives, we will hear when He warns us of danger, we will know the provisions He supplies for us, we will be assured of His care.

Even in times of trouble, we will not be afraid, for we know that He is near to us, and His light will guide us through the darkest of times. Wherever we might go, His love will always surround us and He will lead us through the dark places to where we can be refreshed and spiritually replenished. He nourishes us even in sight of our enemies, for we can sit down in safety where He looks after us. As we follow the Good Shepherd, we know that His love and goodness follow us, that all our needs are met, that we triumph over all the things which are at enmity with our souls, and that peace permeates all that we do, because we dwell with Him forever.

The LORD is my shepherd, I shall not be in want. He makes me lie down in green pastures, he leads me beside quiet waters, he restores my soul. He guides me in paths of righteousness for his name's sake. Even though I walk through the valley of the shadow of death, I will fear no evil, for you are with me; your rod and your staff, they comfort me. You prepare a table before me in the presence of my enemies. You anoint my head with oil; my cup overflows. Surely goodness and love will follow me all the days of my life, and I will dwell in the house of the LORD forever.

Psalm 23

Jesus is the Prince of Peace, and His peace floods our lives as we bring all our cares, concerns and anxieties to Him in prayer. He is able to handle any problem we might face, and more than that, He is able to soothe our troubled minds so that our perspective on anxious situations shifts to heaven's view. We spend so much time trying to change circumstances, when, so often, what is really needed is a change in our own hearts. It has been said that prayer changes not so much the situation, but the one who prays. And through prayer God gives us the strength and the courage we need to face whatever comes our way. Sometimes we face situations that are beyond our ability to change. Then what is most needed is the strength and comfort of the Lord, and His peace which guards our hearts and minds.

There are other situations which do require our intervention, or some kind of action. But before we blunder into a situation, making it worse because of our limited understanding, we should spend some time in prayer, asking God for His wisdom and insight. Then, when we have a clear understanding of the best course of action, we will be able to move confidently and courageously, knowing that God is with us. A prayer life which has been nurtured and cultivated through intimate moments with God prepares us for any crisis or disaster, big or small, which comes our way. And then we can go through life, untroubled by the things of life, confident in His serenity.

*God grant me the serenity to accept the
things I cannot change, the courage to
change the things I can, and the
wisdom to know the difference.
Living one day at a time; enjoying
one moment at a time; accepting
hardship as a pathway to peace.
Taking, as He did, this sinful world
as it is, not as I would have it;
Trusting that He will make all things
right if I surrender to His will;
That I may be reasonably happy in
this life, and supremely happy
with Him forever in the next.*

Reinhold Niebuhr

Corporate praise and worship and corporate prayer have a special place in the life of the believer. Jesus promised, "Where two or three come together in my name, there am I with them" (Mt. 18:20). This does not mean that times alone with God cannot be precious and meaningful, but there is a special power and authority which comes from praying in unity with other believers. We bolster each other's faith, we bear each other's burdens and we delight in the presence of the Lord.

Each day we are aware of new blessings and new mercies which proceed from the hand of the Lord, and each day we sing new, renewed songs of praise to Him. We glorify Him, thanking Him for the great things which He has done on our behalf, and petitioning Him for the great things which He will do. The Lord delights in us, and when we are together with other believers, we are somehow more conscious of that delight. Then our delight in Him also increases, and we realize what a privilege and honor it is to be worshipers of God.

We praise God during times of prayer because, as we do, our focus shifts to Him and to His great love. We remember that He is our Maker and that we are the people of His hand, that He has crowned us with salvation. And our prayers will then be in line with His character and will.

Sing to the LORD a new song,
his praise in the assembly of the saints.
Let Israel rejoice in their Maker;
let the people of Zion be glad
in their King.
Let them praise his name with dancing
and make music to him with
tambourine and harp.
For the LORD takes delight in his
people; he crowns the humble with
salvation. Let the saints rejoice in this
honor and sing for joy on their beds.

Psalm 149:1-5

JABEZ' PRAYER

This little prayer, for so many years skimmed over by so many people, has recently received much attention, but it is still worth looking at yet again. For many years, we have been led to believe that asking God to bless us is a sign of selfishness and immaturity in our Christian lives. Yet God ensured that the Bible preserved a record of the prayer which Jabez prayed, and the result – that He heard and answered. The Bible is full of examples that record God's willingness to bless those who came to Him for blessing. When we ask God to bless us and our endeavors, we ask for His special favor to ensure that we are able to fulfill His purpose and will for our lives.

It is out of the strength and blessing which we receive from God that we are in turn able to bring others to a place of blessing. We know God blesses us in many ways each day, because it is His nature to do so, but each of us has unique issues which God longs for us to bring to Him and discuss with Him. He has a plan and purpose for each one of us, and as we ask for His blessing, He strengthens us and brings us to the place where we are able to do what He calls us to do. The overflow of our hearts and lives blesses others, and if we are walking closely with God, our hearts will be pure, and the blessings we seek will not be for selfish gain, but for extending God's Kingdom. James says that we do not have because we do not ask God, and in this he echoes the words of Jesus: Ask and you will receive. But James warns that our motives in asking will determine the outcome. As we understand the blessings of God, we will find His favor in our lives which will help us to be a blessing to others too.

Jabez cried out to the God of Israel,

"Oh, that you would bless me

and enlarge my territory!

Let your hand be with me,

and keep me from harm so

that I will be free from pain."

And God granted his request.

1 Chronicles 4:10

Jesus said that we are the light of the world, and that we should not hide that light, but let others see how the light changes our hearts and souls, guiding us to do the works of God, so that all men can see the nature of God reflected and rejoice in His goodness (Mt. 5:14-16).

We can only be the light of God in the darkness of the world if we have been lit by the true Light – Jesus Christ (Jn. 9:5). We first need to open the door of our hearts to God, inviting Him in to fellowship with us. Then He will remain in us, and we will be filled with His light and we will be able to do the works He has prepared for us to do. The light of God is lit in our hearts when we first open our hearts to Him, but it can become dim and faint if we allow the things of the world to attract our attention again, and if we neglect the spiritual disciplines, especially prayer and praise. Therefore, we should be careful to keep our hearts open to His influence, ready to fellowship with Him wherever we go in life, developing such intimacy that our love for Him never grows less and that each day we see more and more in Him that calls forth our heartfelt adoration. When a lamp is lit it gives light to the whole house and shines so that all who see it may find their way to the source of that light, Jesus Christ.

Open wide the windows of our spirits,

O Lord, and fill us full of light;

Open wide the door of our hearts,

that we may receive and entertain Thee

with all our powers of

adoration and love. Amen.

Christina Rossetti

A PURE HEART

The prayer of a heart committed to God is to know Him more, to be filled more and more with His love and to know Him more intimately day by day. Jesus said that those who come before God with clean hands and a pure heart will be blessed, for they will see God (Mt. 5:8; Ps. 24:3-4). As we walk with God, our hearts are purified, and His holiness no longer keeps us at a distance from Him. When our hearts are humble, we are open to hearing the whisper of His word, because we no longer insist on our own way. We know that He knows what is best for us in our lives, and so we wait patiently and with humble hearts to hear what He says rather than rushing off to do our own thing.

To serve God effectively and in a way that He cherishes, we need hearts filled with love. He wants us to be obedient to Him because we love Him, not because we feel we have to obey or we will be punished if we don't. As His love increases in our hearts, the value of what we do for Him also increases. We are able to be more effective in His service, because love pulsates through our hearts, and the power of His love stimulates our actions. Hearts filled with faith are able to live as Jesus asks us to, because we know Him whom we believe, and we begin to understand His very nature. He lives in our hearts through faith, and encourages us to do what is right and righteous at all times.

Through prayer, God renews our hearts, filling them with the fruit of His Spirit, and strengthening us to live a life pleasing to Him in every way. Although God is greater than our understanding, as we spend time in prayer we learn to know Him better and better and we find confidence to live out the plans He has made for our lives, because we belong to Him.

Give us
A pure heart, that we may see Thee
A humble heart, that we may hear Thee
A heart of love, that we may serve Thee
A heart of faith, that we may live Thee.
Thou
Whom I do not know, but Whose I am.
Thou
Whom I do not comprehend, but
Who has dedicated me to my fate.
Thou –
Amen.

Dag Hammarskjöld

A GREAT DISTRESS

Sometimes we like to imagine that the Christian life is filled only with the pleasant things in life: sunshine and roses and laughter. But it is true that we live in a world that is at enmity with Christ and while we are citizens of His Kingdom, we are aliens in a world where many things seek to come against us. At times we face things which seem fearful and that drain our strength. It is then that we need to remember that this life is only the preparation for what lies ahead. Nothing that this world hurls at us can defeat us, for we know that we are going on to a better place, and whether we live or die we are with Christ. For us, to live is Christ, to die is gain (Phil. 1:21).

There are not many in the western world who are called to be martyred for their faith, but still we need to be ready, knowing that the salvation of God will not fail and that He will be with us no matter what happens. Bonhoeffer was executed for resisting Hitler's regime during the Second World War. And today, all around the world, people are martyred for their faith in Christ. It is sobering for us who have such freedom to worship God to remember those who have been martyred, and to consider how we would respond should we face such situations. Every day in many ways we are called on to confess Christ before men, and, encouraged by the testimony of those who have been martyred, we can pray that God will strengthen us through His Holy Spirit, so that we will not fail in the day of trial. Let us pray that the grace of God would strengthen us whatever we face.

O Lord, great distress has come
upon me; my cares threaten to crush
me, and I do not know what to do.
O God, be gracious to me and help me.
Give me strength to bear what
You send, and do not let fear rule over
me ... Whether I live or die, I am with
You, and You, My God, are with me.
Lord, I wait for Your salvation
and for Your kingdom. Amen.

Dietrich Bonhoeffer

AN UPWARD FLAME

God comes to hearts that are cold and dead, and sparks a flame that rises up with fire and delight. He ignites our hearts with His fire that burns in us with a holy zeal, inspiring us to great and noble deeds for Him. Our thoughts need to be constantly rising to God, as the flames of a fire reach upwards. Fueled by the passion of God, stoked by His Holy Spirit, consumed by the love of Christ, our minds and hearts are purified in the fire of God's Word. His fire burns ever brighter, and never dims, ever increasing in intensity and rising in heat until we burn as bright flames for Him in a dark, cold world. Prayer keeps our fires burning hot. When we spend time in prayer, our thoughts are centered again on God, and with Him as the center of our lives, all things work together well.

It has often been said that Christianity is a religion of paradoxes – we die to self so that we can be born again, we lose our lives so that we can live forever with God, we give all we have so that we may gain even more. And we give ourselves as slaves to God, so that, being bound to Him, we may know freedom the world can scarcely dream of. God catches us up in the midst of the dreariness of life, creates a new heart in us, and the world becomes a sweet place, filled with the knowledge of Him, perfumed with the fragrance of His presence and pulsating with His life. We do well to concentrate on taking every thought we have in captivity to Jesus Christ (2 Cor. 10:5), for if we leave our thoughts to ramble aimlessly, soon the world seems again a dry and dusty place, void of all that is meaningful. Keep the flame of prayer alive in you, and each day will be filled with splendor and the glory of God.

As flame streams upward,

so my longing thought flies up

with Thee, Thou God and Savior,

who has truly wrought

life out of death, and to us,

loving brought a fresh new world;

and in Thy sweet chains caught

and made us free.

Maurice Egan

Prayer is the school where our spirit is trained to be more like Jesus. And this is a school from which we will not graduate until we one day see Jesus face to face – because it is only when we see Him that we will be like Him (1 Jn. 3:2). Until then, we need to continue diligently in the lessons which He has prepared for us, and which He reveals to us in our times of prayer. As we spend more and more time with Him in prayer, and as our prayer times develop, we find we move from times of simply laying requests before Him – for us and others – and we seek more and more to know His will in all matters. When we spend time in silence before Him, waiting for Him to talk, He will guide our thoughts in ways we did not expect or think possible. He will use our prayer times to help us pray more and more in accordance with His will, because He is conforming us more and more to His image, and so our prayers become more like His. We continue to bring requests to Him, but with a different expectation, a different understanding of how and what He wants to do in and through our lives.

Then, when we go about our daily lives, we carry the sweet fragrance of Him with us, and put into practice that which He has taught us in the secret places in the shadow of His wings. We will proclaim the wonders of His love, which we have discovered for ourselves, to all we meet through the course of our day.

O dear Savior, be not impatient with us – educate us for a higher life, and let that life begin here. May we be always in the school, always disciples, and when we are out in the world may we be trying to put into practice what we have learned at Jesus' feet. What He tells us in the darkness may we proclaim in the light, and what He whispers in our ear in the closets may we sound forth upon the housetops.

Charles Spurgeon

CONSTANT IMPROVEMENT

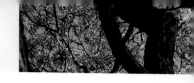

So many people think that God is hard to find, that He is hidden from man, and only through strange mystical experiences can man learn anything of Him. Others believe that God is aloof and distant, angry and disdainful of mankind. They believe that in order to know Him, they need to find all kinds of ways to please Him, so they try and try and try, but somehow do not succeed. The Bible presents a very different picture of God. As we read the Scriptures, we find that God is very eager to reveal Himself to us. In fact, He came to live amongst us so that it would be easy to know Him. He took all our sinfulness on Himself and cast it away as far as the east is from the west, so that all we need to do is accept His free gift of salvation, and come into His presence.

Yet as we approach Him in His unapproachable light, we see more and more clearly our own unworthiness. We realize that salvation only begins when we accept His sacrifice on our behalf. We need to continue to work out our salvation in conjunction with Him. The longer we walk with Jesus, the more we see what is not right in our own lives and characters. At the beginning of our new life, many of the old habits drop off very quickly. The more obvious sins we discard easily. But later on, as we seek to know Him more in prayer, we find faults in our character which are not necessarily visible to the naked eye. It is then that this prayer becomes our prayer – a yearning for constant improvement, a desire to draw closer to God through Christ, and we say, Lord, whatever You need to do, we are happy that You do it, so that we can be fruitful in good works that will glorify God.

We must praise Your goodness,

that You have left nothing undone

to draw us to Yourself. But one thing

we ask of You, our God, not to cease

work on our improvement. Let us

tend towards You, no matter by what

means and be fruitful in good works,

for the sake of Jesus Christ Our Lord.

Ludwig von Beethoven

CONFESSION

It is said that confession is good for the soul. But often we tend to gloss over the wrong things which we do, or the good things which we leave undone. We make excuses for our sin, and forget just how badly our sinful actions affect our relationship with God. When we feel that somehow we aren't getting through to God in prayer, when the heavens feel like brass, and God seems far from us, it may be good to spend some time allowing Him to search our souls and point out those things which are offensive to Him, so that we can ask for His forgiveness, and be cleansed from all unrighteousness. If we are serious about allowing God to change us into the image of Christ, if we truly want to be more like Him, then we need to be aware of those specific things which keep us from moving forward with Him.

True repentance is specific and directed at the things in our own lives which we know have been sinful. We need to admit to God that we know exactly what it is that is keeping us from His purpose in our lives. Sometimes, however, we find it hard to pinpoint the things which are hindering our progress. Then using prayers such as this one can help to highlight issues we might have overlooked. We must allow God to do the prompting in our hearts, laying emphasis on those actions and attitudes which He wants to deal with.

Confession and repentance which is specific, dealing with those things which have "marred the pattern" which God has drawn for our lives, results in our being refreshed, renewed and invigorated so that once again we can live according to God's will for our lives.

If my soul has turned

perversely to the dark;

If I have left some brother

wounded by the way;

If I have preferred my aims to Thine;

If I have been impatient

and would not wait;

If I have marred the pattern

drawn for my life;

If I have cost tears to those I loved;

If my heart has murmured against

Thy will, O Lord, forgive me.

F. B. Meyer

CONSECRATION

God calls us, and we respond to Him. We come to Him with nothing but our pitiful broken beings, and He chooses us to become vessels fit for the Master's use (2 Tim. 2:21). We have nothing which He has not given us, and so we stand before Him with empty hands, but with hearts brimming with the desire to serve Him. Then He fills us with His grace and fashions us into instruments that can contain His glory. We come before Him in humility, consecrating our lives to Him, and He responds by lavishing His love upon us. He comes and takes up residence in our hearts, and He sanctifies every aspect of our lives so that He can use us to advance the gospel in this world.

Everything we have comes from the hand of God. Our gifts and talents are not of our own making, and if we truly desire to honor Him and serve Him, we will surrender those things which we have and which we are to Him so that He can use us as and where He sees fit. Our one desire should be to be used to spread the glory of the knowledge of God wherever we find ourselves. Compelled by His love and with His prayer that our faith fail not, we are fit to be used for whatever purpose and in whatever way He may require. Daily, we should consecrate our lives to Him anew, ready in the strength of His grace, to do whatever He asks us to do.

Use me, my Savior, for
whatever purpose and in whatever
way You may require. Here is my poor
heart, an empty vessel: fill it with
Your grace. Here is my sinful and
troubled soul: quicken it and refresh it
with Your love. Take my heart for
Your abode; my mouth
to spread abroad the glory of
Your name; my love and all my powers
for the advancement of your believing
people, and never allow the
steadfastness and
confidence of my faith to abate.

Dwight L. Moody

Jesus of Nazareth with the Holy Spirit and power, ... went around doing good and healing all who were under the power of the devil, because God was with him (Acts 10:38). When Jesus lived on earth, He set us an example of how we should interact with those people who cross our paths each day. It is in the way we live our daily lives that we most strongly bear testimony of the love of God to others. We are "living epistles" written by the hand of God and sent into the world carrying His message of love and hope to those we meet. Therefore, our words need to be seasoned with salt (Col. 4:6), and flavored with love, so that the people we deal with are blessed by the words we speak. We are ambassadors of Christ, representing Him in love and wisdom to those who do not yet know Him.

Jesus was keenly aware of what was in the hearts and minds of the people He met, and if we develop a deep and abiding relationship with Him, He will help us to have an inkling of what motivates those around us. He will help us to understand their feelings, and so act towards them with kindness and grace. Spending time with Jesus will help us to have time for other people – time to help them when they have needs, time to speak to them with love, time to do little acts of kindness, and to receive their acts of kindness towards us. And so in all these things, we spread the fragrance of Christ because God is with us too.

*O Lord, grant that each one
who has to do with me today may be
the happier for it. Let it be given me
each hour what I shall say, and grant
me the wisdom of a loving heart that I
may say the right thing rightly.
Help me to enter into the mind of
everyone who talks with me and keep
me alive to the feelings of each one
present. Give me a quick eye for
little kindnesses, that I may be ready
in doing them and gracious in
receiving them.
Give me quick perception of the
feelings and needs of others, and make
me eager-hearted in helping them.*

H. M. Soulsby

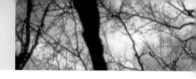

So often we long for grand tasks and exciting challenges where we will be able to bear witness to Christ in spectacular ways. We want to spend our lives on mountaintops and be the instigators of great revivals and world-changing crusades. These are noble longings, but very few are called to such work for God. Of the thousands of Christians who were active in the early church, we know the names of only a few. The ones we do not know of still bore witness to Christ through changed lives lived in loving intimacy with God.

Through the ages, most Christians have been called to serve God through living ordinary lives filled with His extraordinary love. Mothers teach their children to pray, grandfathers live uncompromisingly godly lives, businessmen act with integrity, teachers nurture children in the ways of God. Wherever we find ourselves, God is there and we can live in His presence daily, testifying of His goodness and mercies in all that we do. Whatever we do, whether washing dishes, mowing lawns, driving our cars, working, playing or closing business deals, we need to do it as if we are doing it for Christ. Then every humble act becomes a noble one, and every grand action is humbled in the light of His love.

O God, Thou art with me and it is Thy will that these outward tasks are given me to do. Therefore, I ask Thee, assist me, and through it all let me continue in Thy presence. Be with me in this my endeavor, accept the labor of my hands, fill my heart as always.

Brother Lawrence

The Bible encourages us in many places to wait on the Lord. This, too, is an act of prayer. Some of the most effective prayer times we have are when we sit in silence before the Lord. We have our say, we use all the words we can think of in all the different aspects of prayer, and then we wait. Don't be tempted to come to the end of your words and then rush out of the presence of God. Wait. Wait until you sense that He has finished with you. Sometimes we do not understand exactly what God does in the silences. But we do know that He is present with us and working in us.

As we wait expectantly, we find that He does a deep work in our hearts, rooting up all the qualities in our hearts which hinder the progress of our prayers – the self-centeredness and worldliness and pride which we often don't recognize in our lives, and He replaces these with all that is good and all that is a reflection of His love. He nurtures the fruit of the Spirit in us, pruning what needs to be pruned, and tending the fragile new growth which is pushing through the crustiness of our hearts.

As we wait on Him, we find too that our faith is strengthened, and that our hope in the promises He has made to us is quickened, so that no matter what may try to come against us, our hope in Him will not die. As we wait on Him, we are assured of His steadfast love and eternal goodness, and our strength is renewed. Then when we leave our prayer room strengthened and ready for the day we know that His presence goes with us.

*O Lord, reassure me with Your
quickening Spirit; without You I can
do nothing. Mortify in me all ambition,
vanity, vainglory, worldliness, pride,
selfishness and resistance from
God, and fill me with love, peace,
and all the fruits of the Spirit. O Lord,
I know not what I am, but to You
I flee for refuge.
I would surrender myself to You,
trusting Your precious promises and
against hope believing in hope.
You are the same yesterday, today, and
forever; and therefore, waiting on
the Lord, I trust
I shall at length renew my strength.*

William Wilberforce

DEWS OF QUIETNESS

Life is often lived at a hectic pace. We live in a world which emphasizes personal achievement and success in every area, from health and relationships to business and standards of living. A quick glance at the shelves of bookshops will try to convince you that you can do and be anything you want to do and be – if only you try hard enough. So people put more and more effort into being successful, but somehow never feel that they achieve it. The harder people try to become all they can be, the more stressed they become, and now the new mantra of the world is to find a place of calm in their chaotic lives. The good news is that we, as Christians, can cease from all strivings, asking instead for God to fill us with His peace through Christ and to bring order out of the disordered abyss which modern living tries to plummet us into. We can rest in the finished work of Christ on Calvary.

We do know that our Christian walk is one of constant growth towards maturity, but even in this we have the presence of God through His Holy Spirit to guide and help us, for He leads us into righteousness as we yield to Him. Therefore, we can cease our anxious strivings and allow His peace to calm our troubled minds.

This gentle prayer can help us to find peace in the midst of chaos, serenity in the midst of striving. As He brings order to our lives and peace to our hearts, our lives become a testimony of His peace and beauty to those around us still caught in the web of anxious activity the world weaves. Let His peace and tranquility fall on your heart today, like dew on the early morning grass of a fresh new day.

Drop Thou Thy still

dews of quietness

till all our strivings cease;

Take from our souls

the strain and stress,

And let our ordered

lives confess

the beauty of Thy peace.

J. G. Whittier